AMAZING TENSION GETTERS

56 Real-Life Problems and Predicaments for Today's Youth

David Lynn and Mike Yaconelli

Youth Specialties

ZONDERVAN PUBLISHING HOUSE
Grand Rapids, Michigan

AMAZING TENSION GETTERS
Copyright © 1988 by Youth Specialties, Inc.

Youth Specialties Books are published by the Zondervan Publishing House
1415 Lake Drive, S.E., Grand Rapids, Michigan 49506

Library of Congress Cataloging-in-Publication Data

Lynn, David.
    Amazing tension getters : 53 real-life problems and predicaments for today's youth / David
Lynn & Mike Yaconelli.

    "Youth Specialties."
    ISBN 0-310-34881-1
    1. Teenagers—Religious life. 2. Teenagers—Conduct of life. 3. Church group work with
teenagers. I. Yaconelli, Mike. II. Title.
    BV4531.2.L938 1988
    268'.433—dc19   88−18664
                                                                          CIP
                                                                          AC

Edited by Marilyn McAuley and David Lambert
Designed by Ann Cherryman

Printed in the United States of America

    89 90 91 92 93 94 95 / CH / 12 11 10 9 8 7 6 5 4 3

CONTENTS

These situations have been formulated to cause your youth group to think of all the available options when making a moral choice.

These opinions have been written to reflect the actual feelings of today's adolescents. Your youth group will be asked if they agree or disagree with the statements and to contrast their opinions with the opinions in the book.

The stories in this section require your youth group to rank each character in a story and to provide reasons for those rankings.

These fictional "diary entries" are intimate, no-holds-barred statements of adolescent feelings. Have your youth group read these "confidential" writings and then respond to them.

INDEX BY TOPIC

INTRODUCTION

Today's youth live in a complex and rapidly changing society. Moral standards that once seemed written in stone are now disintegrating. There seem to be no agreed-upon standards and values. As a result, young people are set adrift in a bewildering sea of moral choices without the aid of a moral compass. They are faced daily with an ever-increasing number of options and alternatives without the assistance of a moral roadmap.

In past generations, society agreed upon a widely held set of values. Society rewarded those who went along and penalized those who did not. The cultural norms, more often than not, coincided with biblical norms. Not any longer. Now, young people are being taught that the only norm they can depend on is themselves. "Whatever is right for you" has become the only moral absolute. The result is that moral certainty has been replaced by moral confusion, and the issue in the church has become, "How can we help young people make moral choices in a world that presents so many options?" We are faced with the difficult task of preparing our young people to make right decisions in a culture that no longer cares what is right or wrong.

To put the dilemma of the church in practical terms, we must decide how the church is to deal with the issues of the present in the artificial environment of the Sunday School classroom where options seem black and white. As soon as our young people move out of the classroom, they are faced with complex choices that are neither black nor white. They leave the world of simple solutions and enter the real world of not-so-simple solutions.

Stated simply, the problem is one of transfer. The church needs to provide a learning environment where young people can take what they learn in the classroom and apply it to the world outside. If they cannot transfer what they learn, then it won't be long until they become frustrated and decide to abandon their faith because it does not seem relevant to life. That is why we have published *Tension Getters*, *Tension Getters Two*, and *Amazing Tension Getters*.

These are books of strategies designed specifically to help your young people transfer what they have learned in the classroom to daily life. Each strategy has been chosen for its close resemblance to real-life situations and issues. We hope that when your young people encounter similar situations in the real world, they can transfer the knowledge and skills acquired while using these strategies. Helping young people be prepared for decisions in the real world is the function of *Amazing Tension Getters*. Here's how it works:

Tension Getters Create Tension.

Each strategy in this book has been included because of its potential to create a dilemma or situation with conflicting issues that require young people to think through all possible alternatives and consequences before arriving at a moral decision. Tension is created when there is an overlap of values that make a simple black-and-white response impossible. Most decisions in the real world require sifting through layers of values before a choice is made. For example, let's suppose a young person is asked to help a friend cheat on a test. The student is torn between friendship with the friend, friendship with the other students, the personal value of honesty, and so on. A diagram would look like this:

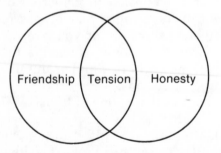

Where these values overlap is the area of tension. A decision must be made in the midst of the reality that all of these values are present at the same time. The issue is to decide which value has priority in the presence of all other values, rather than deciding which one is right or which one is wrong. Recreating this tension helps young people think through their value system and become conscious of its implications in real-life situations.

Tension Getters Require an Atmosphere of Growth.

One of the biggest obstacles to overcome with young people in the church is their preconceived idea that church is where you learn all the right answers. Because we believe the Christian faith is the ultimate answer to the problems of life, young people misunderstand this to mean that it provides a specific answer to each particular problem in life. The Christian faith does provide a foundation upon which young people can deal with the particulars of life, but they must learn how to discover those particulars themselves. For that reason, *Amazing Tension Getters* does not provide answers; it creates questions—the kinds of healthy questions that cause growth.

For growth to occur, it must happen in an atmosphere of neutral openness. That does not mean the leader or the church is neutral on important issues; it simply means that the leader allows the freedom for all points of view to be expressed without judgment. It's important to make the young person feel that what matters more than the right answer is *their* answer. Here's how to create this kind of atmosphere:

1. Open-ended discussion

It's important not to push or force the group's discussion to a conclusion. Certainly the group should stay on the subject, but you don't need to resolve all the loose ends in forty-five minutes. Discussion is squelched when young people feel pressure to end on time and to resolve all issues. The emphasis ought to be on arriving at as many options as possible so that when the decision is made, it is made with all of the alternatives in mind.

2. Freedom to say what one thinks

Young people are often penalized if they say what they really think, especially if what they say is opposed to what the church or the leader thinks. Because this makes them reluctant to express their real feelings, it's important for you to affirm legitimate expressions of opinion no matter what the content. Remember that your allowing young people to say what they believe does not mean that you agree or approve of their ideas. It simply means that you approve of their right to express their ideas and submit them for discussion.

The best response to any comment is to show interest and ask for more. Probe in a nonthreatening manner; ask why they believe the way they do. Push them to follow their idea to their logical consequence; then let those ideas sink or swim on their own merits. If you feel that it's necessary to respond to their ideas, you can always do so later, when giving your concluding remarks.

3. Recreating the realities of life

Three ingredients have to be present in a discussion if you are to simulate a real-life situation:

A. *Situations involving real people*

It's much easier for young people to defend "Tom" than to defend their own personal belief system. They don't feel threatened when discussing other people's beliefs—but, in reality, when they talk about the Tom in the story, they are telling you what *they* believe. Through a story about someone else, they are actually expressing their own value system.

B. *Complex characters*

The characters in *Amazing Tension Getters* have good qualities and bad qualities. There is enough of a mix of good and bad, just like in real life, to make a simplistic response impossible. It's easy to decide who is right when someone is all good like the Lone Ranger, but in real life all people are a mixture of good and bad—like the ordinary people in the strategies in this book.

C. Mixture of consequences

Amazing Tension Getters are constructed in such a way that whatever decisions are made have both good and bad consequences; they help one person while hurting another. That, too, is like life— even the best decisions usually hurt someone.

HOW TO USE TENSION GETTERS

Amazing Tension Getters is participant centered rather than leader centered. If you want to use these strategies successfully, all members of the group need to be encouraged to participate. You must foster a climate that is conducive to discussion by communicating that each person's opinion is worthwhile and that each person has a responsibility within the group to contribute to the solutions. For these strategies to have any meaning, there must be a variety of opinions and viewpoints.

Starting the Discussion

Pass out to each person a copy of the strategy to be discussed, along with a pencil and extra paper for note taking. Instruct the group that the strategy given is the total story—they can't add, subtract, or ask "what if" questions. They're to deal with the story as it is.

When everyone has read the story, divide the group (if it's large enough) into small sections of five to seven. Have each group assign a facilitator* to keep the discussion moving and a recorder to keep a record of the decision made so they can be reviewed or reported to the larger group. Have the facilitator start the discussion by merely asking the questions that accompany the tension getters. The group then discusses the questions and attempts to arrive at one or more conclusions. If a group appears to be stymied, you may want to get them back on the track by throwing out some new ideas, playing the devil's advocate, or attempting to summarize what has already been discussed.

*The facilitator should be one of the young people. If, however, you have several adult youth leaders, you may wish to have each one assigned to a different group. Make sure each leader becomes an equal member of the group. They shouldn't dominate, and if the group looks to the leader for "the answer," have the leader direct the question back to the group.

Ending the Discussion

When all the options have been explored, it's time to make some decisions. If you have more than one group, then each group should arrive at a consensus. If any group can't find a consensus, the members should compile minority reports. Each group should choose someone—perhaps their recorder—to present their report to the larger group.

Allow all views to be shared; allow the larger group to discuss these views after they've been expressed. Now's the time for you to exercise your options about how complicated you want the discussion to become, and how much closure you want to bring to it. You may want to leave the topic hanging until the following week and encourage the young people to talk to their parents or others. This gives the young people time to digest all the implications of the issues raised during the discussion. Or you may want to complicate the discussion by adding new information to the story, such as: "What if Tom were a Christian?" or "What if Linda had only six months to live?" Sometimes, those complications are needed in order to meet the specific needs of your group. There may be times when you want to summarize the discussion and use it as a springboard for a teaching opportunity. Finally, you can allow the questions raised during the discussion to go unanswered, allowing the youth group to wrestle with the issues on their own.

Using Scripture

Each of the strategies in this book is followed by Bible references. These references were selected for their relevance to the particular strategy and for their potential to generate healthy discussion and to stimulate dialogue. They are not to be considered exhaustive. You'll probably think of other applicable passages; feel free to add whatever Scriptures you believe are equally relevant. None of the Scriptures listed are intended to provide "the answer" to the ethical dilemma you're discussing. Instead, they're there to shed light on the situation and to give practical guidance by focusing on the question, "What does God say about this?" It's important not to abuse the Bible by using any of these passages out of context, and it's also important not to deal with the difficult decisions in life without the input of Scripture. The passages listed are just the tip of the iceberg, inviting you to "search the Scriptures" and dig deeper.

Here are some suggestions to help you use the Scripture references effectively:

1. *Read the Scriptures out loud together.* It's important for the group to focus on the Scriptures together so all the members can deal with the biblical implications for the strategy being discussed.

2. *Examine each Scripture separately, checking the context to see what effect it has on the meaning.* Encourage the group to come to an agreement on the meaning of the passage, and then apply that meaning to the strategy you're discussing. Does it have any relevance? How does it affect your decision?

3. *Examine all the Scriptures together; encourage the group to summarize the relationship of the passages.* For example, after reading a number of passages relating to adultery, the group's summary statement might be, "Although God is against adultery, he also seems to treat the adulterer with love." Apply your summary statement to the strategy you are discussing. How does it affect your decision?

Be prepared for the fact that some Scriptures will actually make the decision-making process more difficult. There are many Scriptures that seem to present opposing viewpoints on the same issue. Whether that's true or not, we have not used Scripture as a gimmick. We have tried to honestly present relevant Scriptures (whether they speak clearly or vaguely) with the knowledge that "all Scripture is profitable," and that God's Word "will not return to him void."

WHEN TO USE TENSION GETTERS

Amazing Tension Getters is not a curriculum. It isn't designed to be used every week—in fact, it's most effective when it's used to supplement the larger unit of curriculum you're using. It isn't a book full of gimmicks or quickie programs that will keep your young people busy for an hour. But this book full of individual strategies that can stand alone or be used with others can meet a variety of needs if used properly. Here are some suggestions.

Discussion Starters

A primary function of *Amazing Tension Getters* is to create lively discussion. Each strategy is a story, and almost all of them relate to situations similar to those your young people encounter every day. As a result, you can expect high interest. In other words, rather than beginning your youth meeting with "What do you think about cheating?" you can start with a story about Tom, the school jock, who asks a friend to help with an upcoming test. Everyone in your youth group will have an opinion.

Spiritual Thermometer

As you observe the discussion generated by *Amazing Tension Getters*, you can discover, in a nonthreatening atmosphere, what your young people believe. By observing them during the entire process of decision making, you can know not only what the kids in your youth group believe but how they got there. This is invaluable for the youth leader who wants to know his or her students and understand what their needs are. If the content of your program is based on the needs of your youth, *Amazing Tension Getters* should become an integral part of your program.

These strategies are also effective in helping your young people discover what they really believe. "The Island Affair" (page 113 in the first volume of *Tension Getters*) was used at a young-adult conference a few years back. Before the strategy was used, the conferees were asked if they believed in situational ethics. Not one person admitted that he or she did. After discussing "The Island Affair" (which involves the issues of situational ethics), over fifty percent of the conference realized that they did believe in situational ethics, at least in this instance. This knowledge was not only invaluable for the conferees themselves, but also for the leaders who could then focus on that particular issue.

Creative Alternatives

Although *Amazing Tension Getters* is full of strategies that are great discussion starters, there are many other possibilities. You can use these strategies to introduce a role play, to stimulate some creative writing, or to set the scene for a skit or dramatic situation. The possibilities are endless once kids are motivated.

You will find one other advantage to these strategies: They create tangent issues. Because these strategies deal with many different values at the same time, you will often find your young people talking about something other than the main topic. In the process of the discussion, they have focused on a tangent issue. Sometimes, you'll want to get them back to the main topic, but often you'll want to pursue the tangent issue because it expresses a need you weren't aware of.

CAUTION

Remember that you are the final authority when it comes to programing for your youth group. You are the one who must decide whether your group needs more tension at this time, whether they are mature enough to hear all the alternatives, and whether they are spiritually able to deal with conflict. Here are some guidelines to keep in mind:

1. *Know your kids well.* Some young people are not ready to handle certain problems. You might have planned to discuss the issue of death, but because one of your young people has a parent who is dying, it may not be the time to discuss that subject. It might also be the perfect time—but to make that decision you have to know your kids well.

2. *Don't dump on kids.* There are many issues of our faith that are difficult for even adults to handle. Be careful not to shoot holes through all of their arguments just to create conflict. As young people mature, they not only learn more, but they learn to handle more ambiguity. Make sure your young people are getting a lot of positive content along with content that creates tension.

3. *Don't try to shock kids for effect.* If you play the devil's advocate, make sure your arguments are sensible. In other words, don't become so artificial in your role as spoiler that the kids don't take your point of view seriously. Sometimes leaders try to shock kids with extreme arguments or positions that, more often than not, have a reverse effect. The kids treat the discussion more like a skit and the discussion degenerates into a meaningless exchange.

4. *Give people time.* Don't feel that every issue must be resolved in sixty minutes. Let the young people go home thinking. Let issues stay unresolved for a while. It takes time to think through issues, and when young people are carrying unresolved issues, they usually end up talking with someone about them, like their parents or friends. That dialogue can be very productive.

5. *Don't be afraid of controversy or failure.* When you create tension, deal with controversial issues, send people home with issues

unresolved, or disturb beliefs that people are comfortable with, you are going to generate criticism from young people as well as from parents. Sometimes the criticism will be justified, because sometimes you will make mistakes. Sometimes you may even lose a young person, but those are the risks of good education. Admit your mistakes, learn from your failures, but don't back off simply because you have pushed people into new areas of growth and maturity.

We think you will find *Amazing Tension Getters* an invaluable resource. Enjoy this book. Use it wisely, selectively, and prayerfully. We hope you will find it to be a significant contribution to your youth group's spiritual growth and development.

SECTION ONE

OPTIONS

These situations have been formulated to cause your youth group to think of all the available options when making a moral choice. Your group will be asked to choose one particular option over the others and explain why that option was chosen.

1 ■ VIOLENT DILEMMA

Susan is totally confused. She has known for a long time that her father physically abuses her mother, but she has felt helpless to do anything. Susan's mother absolutely refuses to talk about it and doesn't allow Susan to tell anyone. "I love your father, and if you tell someone, it might mean your father would go to jail." Well, Susan doesn't want her father to go to jail, nor does she want to cause her mother any more pain.

But Susan is sixteen now, and last night was too much. Her father came home in a very ugly mood; he not only beat her mother severely, but he also tried to hurt Susan. She ran out of the house and came to you. She wants to know what to do.

▶ What are Susan's options?

▶ What would you advise her to do? Why?

 Scripture Guide: Exodus 20:12   Romans 12:17—21
                   Matthew 15:4   Ephesians 6:1
                   Romans 12:12   Colossians 3:20

2 ■ CHRISTMAS IN HAWAII

Paula's parents have been divorced for five years now. Her father has remarried and lives out of the area. Paula lives with her mother and sees her father once or twice a year. Her mother has never remarried. Now that Paula is in high school, she notices that her mother is increasingly uncomfortable with Paula's trips to see her father. Her mother has never made an issue out of the trips—until now.

To make things worse, Paula has been invited to go to Hawaii with her father and stepmother during the Christmas school break. Paula's mother doesn't want her to go. She says she will have to spend Christmas all alone—and after all the horrible things her father has done, *he* is the one who should be alone. All Paula knows is that she loves her mother *and* her father and wouldn't want to hurt either of them. She comes to you for advice.

 What are Paula's options?

 What would you advise her to do? Why?

● Scripture Guide: Malachi 4:5–6   Ephesians 6:1
                    Romans 12:8–10   Colossians 3:20

3 ■ BIG SISTER/BIG PROBLEM

Belinda's sister is ruining her life.

Belinda is fifteen and her sister, Teresa, is twenty-one. Teresa is severely mentally retarded. Because Belinda's parents both work, she ends up having to take care of Teresa a lot. Belinda knows she shouldn't feel resentment, but she does. She wishes her parents would put Teresa in a special home, but they say they don't have enough money. The way Teresa acts embarrasses Belinda and her friends. Belinda can tell her friends don't like to come over anymore. In fact, Belinda sometimes feels like her friends wonder about *her*.

Belinda feels more than resentment—she is beginning to hate her sister. She knows she needs to do something. She comes to you for help.

▶ What are Belinda's options?

▶ What would you advise her to do? Why?

 Scripture Guide: Matthew 5:43−44   Romans 12:10
                    John 5:35   Romans 13:10
                    John 15:13   James 4:6
                    Romans 12:3−8

4 ■ FAMILY TIES

Ricardo's family has seen noticeable changes in his life since he became a Christian. He has stopped running around with the wrong crowd. His grades are beginning to improve. Overall, the improvement is great— except for one problem.

Ricardo's family is very close. They have always spent a great deal of time together. But now that Ricardo is involved in the church, he's gone all the time—Sunday morning, Sunday night, Wednesday night, and almost every weekend at some church activity. When Ricardo is home, the family is uncomfortable. Mom and Dad watch their language, and everyone is uneasy, waiting for Ricardo to say something religious.

Ricardo's parents have told him that they don't mind his new faith, as long as he keeps it to himself. But they do mind his being gone so much. They feel that he has become a stranger in the house, and that he's losing touch with his brothers and sisters. So, last night, they told him that he has to cut back on church activities and stay home during the week. He can attend church once on Sunday, and that's all.

Ricardo was crushed. He not only *wants* to go to the youth activities, he *needs* them. He knows that if he quits going, he'll be right back where he was a few months ago. He comes to you for help.

▶ What are Ricardo's options?

▶ What would you advise him to do? Why?

● Scripture Guide: Malachi 4:5–6 John 13:16
Matthew 10:37 Acts 5:29
Matthew 15:4 Ephesians 6:4
Luke 14:26

5 ■ SHOULD GOD PLAY THE LOTTERY?

Some dads fish, some dads hunt, but Gary's dad gambles. For as long as Gary can remember, Mr. Garner has taken his family to the horse races in the summer and to Las Vegas in the winter. Most of the time his dad would lose—only up to a certain amount, and then he would quit. But every once in awhile he would win, and those were wonderful times. Gary's dad would take the whole family out to dinner, and there would be a big family celebration with surprise gifts for everyone.

Gary's family is active in a local church. A week ago, he was invited to a friend's church to hear a guest speaker. The topic of his sermon was, "Why God Dislikes Gambling." Gary was really surprised. It had never occurred to him that gambling might be wrong. Gary knew there were people who were addicted to gambling, and he understood how it could be wrong for some people—but this speaker was saying that *no* Christian should gamble. Ever. For any reason. Now Gary is confused. He comes to you for advice.

▶ What are Gary's options?

▶ What would you advise him to do? Why?

● Scripture Guide: Matthew 6:24–34   Hebrews 13:5
                      2 Thessalonians 3:10–13   1 John 2:15–17
                      1 Timothy 6:6–11

6 ■ OLDER MAN—YOUNGER WOMAN

Melissa is a freshman at San Anselmo High School. She's fifteen, but looks much older. Her mother has made it clear that Melissa can't date senior guys, and that has never been a problem—until now. Gordie is a total babe. He's also a Christian, active in Young Life, and a great guy.

Melissa isn't the type to sneak around. She and her mom have a great relationship, and she feels sure her mom will understand. So Melissa asks her mom if she can go out with Gordie. The answer is no.

Melissa can't believe it. Her mom won't listen to reason. Melissa wants to do what her mom says, and she doesn't want to damage their relationship, but she *doesn't* want to lose Gordie. She comes to you for help.

▶ What are Melissa's options?

▶ What would you advise her to do? Why?

 Scripture Guide: Ephesians 6:1–2   Colossians 3:20
                     Ephesians 6:4

7 ■ WHOM TO TELL?

Fifteen months ago Denise had an abortion. It was an emotionally horrifying experience that took Denise almost a year of counseling to get over. Denise now feels that abortion is wrong and believes that God has forgiven her. She has been trying to get on with her life.

For the past few months, Denise has been getting pretty serious with a new guy, Graham. He's great—one of those rare guys nowadays who has standards. They've had some wonderful talks, and Graham has made it clear what he thinks about abortion. He hates the thought of it.

Denise is miserable because the more serious she gets with Graham, the more she feels the need to tell him what she's done. He might find out anyway—her old boyfriend knows, and her best girlfriend knows. They've been sworn to secrecy, but you never know. And if Graham found out from someone else, well, that could be a disaster. Denise comes to you for advice.

▶ What are Denise's options?

▶ What would you advise her to do? Why?

 Scripture Guide: Romans 4:7–8   James 5:16
                    2 Corinthians 5:17

8 ■ GOOD FRIEND TO A BAD FRIEND

Samantha and Crista have been good friends for a long time. But Samantha has changed over the last year, and not for the better. She has dropped out of church, started working at a fast-food place, bought a car, taken up smoking, and is known to drink quite a bit at parties. She's still the bubbly, fun person she always was. She says that she's outgrown the church and all that religion stuff, but that nothing else has changed. That isn't quite true—everyone else has seen the change in Samantha, including her parents and Crista's parents, and no one likes it.

Samantha's parents are concerned and have asked Crista to stick with Samantha and try to help her. That was fine with Crista—until last week, when her parents sat her down and said they didn't want her hanging around Samantha anymore. They thought Samantha was a bad influence on her. Crista had to admit to herself that Samantha had influenced her negatively lately, but not enough to be a problem. Crista doesn't know what to do. She wants to be Samantha's friend, but her parents say absolutely not. Crista comes to you for advice.

▶ What are Crista's options?

▶ What would you advise her to do? Why?

● Scripture Guide: Proverbs 1:8   Ephesians 6:1–2
                     Proverbs 4:18–19   Colossians 3:20
                     Romans 12:16

9 ■ THE BOY WHO WOULDN'T GIVE UP

Jill and Gordon had been going together for three years. From the beginning, Jill knew the relationship had problems, but she kept thinking that either they'd break up or things would get better. But things didn't get better, nor did they break up. Gordon became more and more possessive and demanding. Finally, when Jill graduated from high school, she told Gordon it was over. Gordon was blown away—he had thought they were getting married. He cried, pleaded, and became very angry, but Jill stuck to her decision.

Then Gordon began calling her at home every night and at work every morning. Jill refused to talk to him. He would follow her home from work and try to talk to her. One night at 2:00 A.M., Jill heard a scratching at her window. It was Gordon. Jill called her father and he firmly convinced Gordon that coming around at 2 A.M. was not a good idea. Still Gordon persisted.

Then Jill got the letter. Gordon said that he loved her very much. He said he couldn't understand how she could have initiated their sexual involvement and now act like that didn't matter. He closed by telling Jill that if she didn't come back to him, he didn't know what he would do. He might even kill himself. It was up to her. The letter hurt Jill. She certainly didn't want to be responsible for Gordon taking his life. She comes to you for advice.

▶ What are Jill's options?

▶ What would you advise her to do?

● Scripture Guide: Proverbs 18:22   1 Corinthians 6:18

10 ■ LITTLE SISTER

It's tough when you're the first child. Especially if you're a girl. Your parents try to keep you from growing up for as long as they can. Lauren can still remember every fight she had with her parents about growing up. A fight when she wanted to wear panty hose, a fight when she wanted to wear makeup, a fight over getting pierced ears, then a fight over the size of her earrings. But now her little sister, Leslie, is growing up and she gets to do anything she wants. She's just twelve, and already she's wearing lip gloss, big earrings, and high heels. She looks like a miniature twenty year old. Lauren has brought this up to her parents several times, but they deny that Leslie is getting away with anything. Lauren is resentful and feels cheated. Now her parents are telling her she can't drive alone until she's eighteen. Lauren blows up at her parents and leaves home. She comes to your house. She wants to know what to do.

▶ What are Lauren's options?

▶ What would you advise her to do? Why?

 Scripture Guide: Deuteronomy 11:19–20 Ephesians 6:1
 Esther 1:22 Ephesians 6:4

11 ■ HUNCHBACK

Stacy kept staring at the mirror. She had known for the last few months that something was wrong, but she hadn't been able to figure out what. Now she knew. There was something very wrong with her back. Her shoulders weren't even, and her back seemed to have a slight curve to it. Stacy wanted to believe that it was just an illusion, that she was being a hypochondriac—but she couldn't deny it anymore.

Stacy told her parents. After the doctor's examination, he explained that about 10 percent of all teenagers have some form of scoliosis, or curvature of the spine. He explained that if Stacy would wear a brace for three years, the scoliosis could be eliminated—or at least slowed to the point that no one would notice. But Stacy would have to wear the brace religiously. Then the doctor showed her the brace. It was horrible. Stacy began to cry. There went the beach, the bikinis, sports. She would look like a freak for three years. Stacy made up her mind right then that she would not wear that brace. God could make it so that she didn't have to wear the brace—he could heal her. Certainly he wouldn't want her to look like a freak during her sophomore, junior, and senior years, would he? She comes to you for advice.

▶ What are Stacy's options?

▶ What would you advise her to do?

 Scripture Guide: Mark 10:27   Luke 1:37
Mark 14:36   1 Peter 2:13

12 ■ THE LONER

Don wasn't stupid. He knew what everyone thought of him. The mirror doesn't lie—Don wasn't very good looking. Ha! That was a laugh; he was just plain weird looking. Everyone made fun of him. He wished he could say, "Well, I may be weird looking, but at least I get straight A's" or "Go ahead, don't be friends with me. I'll drive my Porsche by myself." But Don's folks didn't have much money and his grades were average. Don was just your basic no-one-wants-to-be-around-you type of guy. He was lonely. All Don wanted was a friend. That wasn't too much to ask for, was it? Don was very lonely—and, since you're in his geometry class, and since you're the only one in class who even acts like he exists, he comes to you for advice.

▶ What are Don's options?

▶ What would you advise him to do? Why?

 Scripture Guide: Matthew 5:46   John 13:34
                      Matthew 19:19   Philippians 2:3–4
                      Matthew 22:39   James 1:9

SECTION TWO

OPINIONS

These opinions have been written to reflect the actual feelings of many of today's adolescents. Your youth group will be asked if they agree or disagree with the statements and to contrast their opinions with the opinions in the book.

13 ■ THIS CAN'T BE HAPPENING

I can't believe it. My parents are getting a divorce. My mom says it's because Dad's working all the time and doesn't care about her. But what about me? It seems like *neither* of them cares about me. Why do they have to do this *now*? It really screws up my high-school years. They could have waited until I was out of the house and in college. Sure, I knew they weren't happy, but so what? At least *I* was happy. Now we're *all* unhappy. Besides, they can move or get another job, but what can I do? Change schools my senior year? Get a job? Give me a break. I am really angry at my parents for being so selfish that they can't even think of their own child and what this is doing to him.

Rick, 18, Senior

How do you feel about Rick's statement?

Strongly Agree	Agree	Neutral	Disagree	Strongly Disagree

▶ If you agree, what would you add to the statement above?

▶ If you disagree, why?

● Scripture Guide: Genesis 2:24   Ephesians 6:4
                    Matthew 5:31–32   Colossians 3:21
                    Ephesians 6:2   1 Timothy 3:2–5

14 ■ COVER UP

Hey, I'm not weird. I like a good-looking girl as much as anyone else. I mean, I'm going with Jennifer, the all-time greatest looking girl in our high school. She has a great body. But I'm not going with her just because of her body; I like *her*. But I know how guys think, so I watch what she wears in public. I don't let her wear a bikini; I don't let her wear halter tops, either. My friends think I'm stupid and conservative. They like seeing girls foxing out in sexy clothes, but they would never want to go with a girl like that.

Ed, 17, Junior

How do you feel about Ed's statement?

Strongly Agree	Agree	Neutral	Disagree	Strongly Disagree

▶ If you agree, what would you add to the statement above?

▶ If you disagree, why?

 Scripture Guide: Matthew 5:28   1 Peter 3:3–5
                   Matthew 7:1–2   1 Timothy 2:9–10

15 ■ CHANGE OF MIND

When I was in junior high, I thought people who took drugs were stupid. I still do if you're talking about stoners. But now that I'm in high school I think drugs are just like anything else—if you abuse them they're bad; if you don't abuse them, they can be okay. I smoke a joint now and then, but not during school or when I'm driving, or even every time there's a party. Just once in awhile. It's not as bad as everyone says. My parents would totally flip out if they knew I had *ever* smoked before. But, hey, they drink and it ain't no big deal.

Steve, 18, Senior

How do you feel about Steve's statement?

Strongly Agree	Agree	Neutral	Disagree	Strongly Disagree

▶ If you agree, what would you add to the statement above?

▶ If you disagree, why?

 Scripture Guide: Joel 1:5   1 Corinthians 6:12
                                 1 Corinthians 3:16–20

16 ■ BE TRUE TO YOUR FRIENDS

Look. Everyone lies. It's just part of being a teenager. If by lying you can keep your folks happy and keep your school and your life under control, then why not? I don't mean that it's okay to lie all the time. And I don't think you should lie to your friends, because once you do that and your friends find out—well, you won't have any friends. Here's the way I look at it. When you're in high school, everyone's on your case—your parents, your teachers, your boss at work—and you *have* to lie to keep them off your back. The only protection you and I have against all that pressure is to lie once in a while.

Brenda, 17, Junior

How do you feel about Brenda's statement?

Strongly Agree	Agree	Neutral	Disagree	Strongly Disagree

▶ If you agree, what would you add to the statement above?

▶ If you disagree, why?

● Scripture Guide: Exodus 20:16   Proverbs 19:22
Proverbs 19:5   John 8:44–47

17 ■ NEVER ADMIT MORE THAN THEY KNOW

Here's my philosophy. When your mom or dad, a teacher, or some other adult confronts you or starts questioning you about something they think you've done, deny it all first. Then, if they confront you with some obvious fact, admit to that, but nothing else. Deny everything else. For example, if my folks came in and confronted me because I got in late the night before, the discussion would go something like this:

Parents: What time did you get in last night, Craig? You were supposed to be home at midnight.

Craig: I *was* home at midnight—or maybe ten minutes after. I didn't look at my watch.

Parents: It must have been more than ten minutes, Craig, because I woke up at 12:45 and checked and you still weren't home.

Craig: Well, it *might* have been that late, but I know I left the party way before twelve so I'd be home on time.

Parents: Was there any drinking going on at the party?

Craig: I sure didn't see any.

Parents: Mrs. Johnson said she had to send a whole bunch of guys away from the party who had stashed some booze in the front bushes and were drinking out on the front lawn.

Craig: Maybe—I don't know. I was inside the house the whole time.

It's a great strategy. It works every time. Only admit what they know and deny everything else.

Craig, 17, Junior

How do you feel about Craig's statement?

| Strongly Agree | Agree | Neutral | Disagree | Strongly Disagree |

▶ If you agree, what would you add to the statement above?

▶ If you disagree, why?

 Scripture Guide: Proverbs 19:22   1 John 2:3—6
                               1 Timothy 1:8—11

18 ■ MELLOW FELLOW

I think this Christian stuff is cool. Seriously, I think it's great—as long as you don't get too weird about it. I like Young Life; it's a lot of fun. And I love youth group. We have a great youth worker and a super neat program at our church, and that's all great. But when they start saying we ought to tell our friends about God all the time, and go to church every week, and go to the mission field—come on, who's got time for that stuff? You can do that when you're older. Besides, as long as youth group, or Young Life, or church keeps you off the streets and gives you a good time, what else do you need? If someone wants to be a minister some day, great; but I don't think I should feel guilty just because I don't want to. When you're in high school, you have a lot to do—and church ought to be a part of what you do; but that's it, only a part. Life is a lot more than going to church.

Roger, 16, Sophomore

How do you feel about Roger's statement?

Strongly Agree	Agree	Neutral	Disagree	Strongly Disagree

▶ If you agree, what would you add to the statement?

▶ If you disagree, why?

● Scripture Guide: Matthew 28:19–20   1 Peter 2:5
Hebrews 9:27   Revelation 15:4
Hebrews 10:25

19 ■ WHAT'S IMPORTANT

You know what's important? I'll tell you. Making the bucks. That always makes people mad when I say that, but they only get mad because it's true. Making a living, that's it. That's the bottom line. You gotta have money to buy a car, have nice clothes, get an apartment or a house, and do fun things. That's what life is about. Who runs the country? Who runs the churches? Who runs everything? The people with the bucks, that's who. Anyone who tells you anything else is a liar.

Connor, 16, Sophomore

How do you feel about Connor's Statement?

Strongly Agree	Agree	Neutral	Disagree	Strongly Disagree

▶ If you agree, what would you add to the statement above?

▶ If you disagree, why?

● Scripture Guide: Matthew 6:19–21 Matthew 19:21
Matthew 6:24 1 Timothy 6:10
Matthew 6:25–34

20 ■ NUCLEAR PIE

To listen to all these adult sociologist types talk, you would think all the teenagers in the world were sitting around totally afraid that the bomb is going to drop. What a joke. None of my friends sit around worrying about a nuclear holocaust. They *do* worry they won't get their piece of the pie, but that's about it. We're not anti-nuclear as much as we are anti-anything that keeps us from living the good life. All we care about is that we get to grow up and have a good time; whatever keeps us from doing that, we're against.

Serena, 15, Sophomore

How do you feel about Serena's statement?

| Strongly Agree | Agree | Neutral | Disagree | Strongly Disagree |

▶ If you agree, what would you add to the statement above?

▶ If you disagree, why?

● Scripture Guide: Matthew 6:19–20   Matthew 6:25–34

21 ■ NEGATIVE OUTLOOK

Every time I do something wrong, my parents remind me of all the things I've done wrong in the last two years. They never forget and seldom forgive. They always focus on the negative. I can do everything I am supposed to for three weeks in a row and they never say a word, but make one mistake and I never stop hearing about it. I don't think they've ever said a positive thing to me. It doesn't matter what I do—they're never satisfied.

Arlin, 14, Freshman

How do you feel about Arlin's statement?

Strongly Agree	Agree	Neutral	Disagree	Strongly Disagree

▶ If you agree, what would you add to the statement above?

▶ If you disagree, why?

● Scripture Guide: Ephesians 6:4   Hebrews 8:12
                    Colossians 3:21

22 ■ IT'S MY BODY

It's *my* body. I don't understand why my parents think they can tell me what to do with my body. I'm old enough now to know what's good for me and what isn't. Besides, I usually don't get in arguments with my folks about what's *good* for me; it's usually just a matter of taste. And my taste is just as "right" as theirs. When it comes to my hairstyle, my earring, or any other part of my personal appearance, I think that should be *my* choice, not my parents'.

Seth, 15, Sophomore

How do you feel about Seth's statement?

Strongly Agree	Agree	Neutral	Disagree	Strongly Disagree

▶ If you agree, what would you add to the statement above?

▶ If you disagree, why?

● Scripture Guide: Exodus 21:17   Malachi 4:6
Proverbs 22:6   Colossians 3:20

23 ■ I DON'T WANT TO DIE

I don't care what they say in church about heaven, I don't want to die. It may be great up there, but I like it here just fine. I don't want to go to heaven right now. I don't want to sit around with a bunch of angels. I want to live and have fun right now. If that means I'm not a Christian, then I guess I'm not a Christian. Because I don't think anyone should want to die rather than live.

Kendra, 16, Sophomore

How do you feel about Kendra's statement?

| Strongly Agree | Agree | Neutral | Disagree | Strongly Disagree |

▶ If you agree, what would you add to the statement above?

▶ If you disagree, why?

 Scripture Guide   Genesis 3:1–5   Philippians 1:21–24
                                 Luke 12:18–21   Hebrews 9:27

24 ■ DON'T KNOCK ROCK

I can't believe so many adults get bent out of shape over rock music. I'll bet 99 percent of the kids never even listen to the words. I don't. I might even know the words to some songs by heart, but I still don't really think about them that much. Oh, yeah, sure, there are some heavy metal freaks running around with Iron Maiden and AC/DC T-shirts, but I don't think they listen to the words either.

Cal, 18, Senior

How do you feel about Cal's statement?

Strongly Agree	Agree	Neutral	Disagree	Strongly Disagree

▶ If you agree, what would you add to the statement above?

▶ If you disagree, why?

● Scripture Guide: 2 Samuel 6:14   Ephesians 5:19–20
                     Psalms 149:3   Philippians 4:8

25 ■ SEX IS FOR EVERYONE

Nobody waits until they're married to have sex anymore. Nobody. Except maybe somebody who grew up on an island where there wasn't anybody of the opposite sex—or maybe somebody who lies a lot. Sure, you have to be careful—but having sex is just a normal part of relationships nowadays.

Jean, 17, Junior

How do you feel about Jean's statement?

Strongly Agree	Agree	Neutral	Disagree	Strongly Disagree

▶ If you agree, what would you add to the statement above?

▶ If you disagree, why?

● Scripture Guide: 1 Corinthians 6:9   2 Corinthians 12:21
                    1 Corinthians 6:12–13 Galatians 5:19
                    1 Corinthians 9:27

26 ■ AFTER SEX, THEN WHAT?

I had sex with this guy. It wasn't great, but I still liked it. Anyway, I felt guilty about it and I asked God to forgive me. I even broke up with the guy. My youth leaders told me that God did forgive me, and that I should never do it again. I *know* I shouldn't have sex again, but every time I go out with a new guy I want to. I can't help it. I've tried to keep from having sex, but once you've experienced it, you can't exactly go back to holding hands. Anyone who thinks you can have sex and then not have it anymore is crazy.

Tina, 16, Junior

How do you feel about Tina's statement?

| Strongly Agree | Agree | Neutral | Disagree | Strongly Disagree |

▶ If you agree, what would you add to the statement above?

▶ If you disagree, why?

● Scripture Guide: Romans 8:5–8   Galatians 5:19
1 Corinthians 6:12–20

27 ■ PICKY PARENTS

My parents are paranoid. Every time I come home from a party they want to know if there was any drinking or drugs. Well, of course there was. You can't go to a party anymore without someone drinking or smoking dope, but that doesn't mean I do it, or even want to. I don't drink and I don't do drugs. My folks should believe me. If my parents knew what half of my friends did, they wouldn't let me have anything to do with them. But I can't tell my parents what really goes on; they'd lock me in chains and only let me out of the house to go to school and back. I wish they could just understand that they can trust me, and that what my *friends* do doesn't affect what *I* do.

Connor, 15, Sophomore

How do you feel about Connor's statement?

Strongly Agree	Agree	Neutral	Disagree	Strongly Disagree

▶ If you agree, what would you add to the statement above?

▶ If you disagree, why?

 Scripture Guide: Matthew 7:1–5   Ephesians 6:10–12
Ephesians 5:8–13

28 ■ TAKE THIS JOB AND SHOVE IT

I work for this fast-food place. I make minimum wage, just like everybody else. My boss treats me like dirt. I get the worst jobs, and he's always yelling at me for every little mistake. If I need a day or a weekend off to do something with my family, he won't give it to me. Look, I'm only in high school. This isn't my life's work. I'm not sitting around dreaming of becoming a professional fast-food employee. I'm just working to get some spending money. And they're getting real cheap help. They know that. They shouldn't try to take advantage of me by acting like they're doing me a favor. I'm doing *them* a favor.

I asked for this next weekend off to go water-skiing, and my boss said no—so I quit. There are plenty of other fast-food places always looking for help.

Ron, 16, Sophomore

How do you feel about Ron's statement?

| Strongly Agree | Agree | Neutral | Disagree | Strongly Disagree |

▶ If you agree, what would you add to the statement above?

▶ If you disagree, why?

 Scripture Guide:　Psalms 103:5　　　　Ephesians 6:5–8
　　　　　　　　　　　　Ecclesiastes 11:9

55

29 ■ SCHOOL IS NO BIG DEAL

My parents are more concerned about how I do in school than anything else in my life. They're always pressuring me to take college-prep courses and get straight A's. Well, I don't feel that way. School is okay and I'm smart enough to get decent grades, but I'm tired of the pressure. So my SAT's aren't great, so what? I can always go to junior college or not go to college at all for a while. In fact, a bunch of my friends and I are talking about traveling around Europe for a year after we graduate from high school. Our parents are totally freaking out at that idea. Why? I don't think you learn all that much in high school anyway. Besides, most of the teachers couldn't care less about education. They just collect their paycheck. I just don't think you need to panic about grades. I'll get serious about school later. Right now I want to enjoy my high-school years.

Linda, 18, Senior

How do you feel about Linda's statement?

| Strongly Agree | Agree | Neutral | Disagree | Strongly Disagree |

▶ If you agree, what would you add to the statement above?

▶ If you disagree, why?

 Scripture Guide: Proverbs 1:4   Ecclesiastes 12:12
                    Proverbs 1:22   1 Timothy 4:12
                    Proverbs 3:13

30 ■ PHONY KIDS

High school kids are so phony. You go to a class or conference on racism or hunger, and kids sit around crying and saying how concerned they are. Then when the class is over, you see the same kids making fun of some other kid and talking about all the new clothes they "need" right now. My friends only care about themselves. They *say* they're not going to be like their parents, that they are going to care about the world, and hunger, and nuclear war—but as soon as school's over, they're back to thinking about themselves full-time. None of my friends think a thing about inconveniencing their parents or asking for more money. In fact, they get mad if their parents won't go out of their way to help them. We're a bunch of spoiled, selfish, self-centered little brats. We pretend to care about the world, but really we don't care about anything except money, clothes, our friends, our music, and having a good time.

Claudia, 18, Senior

How do you feel about Claudia's statement?

| Strongly Agree | Agree | Neutral | Disagree | Strongly Disagree |

▶ If you agree, what would you add to the statement above?

▶ If you disagree, why?

● Scripture Guide: Ecclesiastes 3:1–8   Matthew 6:25–34
                      Ecclesiastes 12:1   Matthew 19:16–26

31 ■ OLD-FASHIONED

I guess I'm old-fashioned, but I really do think there's a hell. I believe that my friends need to accept Jesus. I don't want them to go to hell. I don't think I'm better than they are, and I don't think they're horrible people—I just care about them. I'm one of those weirdos that loves God. I care about my friends. I worry about them. I know that people who don't believe in Christ may be nice people, but they are never going to be happy without him. Even though people make fun of me, I think I should try to tell all my friends about Jesus. And if they don't like it, that's all right—they still need to hear about him.

Bruce, 15, Freshman

How do you feel about Bruce's statement?

Strongly Agree	Agree	Neutral	Disagree	Strongly Disagree

▶ If you agree, what would you add to the statement above?

▶ If you disagree, why?

● Scripture Guide: Luke 13:5   Hebrews 10:35–39
John 3:16   2 Peter 3:8–10
Hebrews 9:27   1 John 2:17

32 ■ THE BEAUTIFUL PEOPLE

I go to this humongous church. It is *the* place to go. We have like five thousand members and about two hundred high-school kids in the youth group. All the kids in the group are really popular at school. Our youth worker is Mr. Stud—good looking, athletic, good speaker. We have the greatest programs and the greatest camps. We have lots of money in our youth budget and the adults in the church really support us. We have a lot of really neat mission projects, too.

There's just one problem. The whole thing is a fraud. Maybe joke is a better word. I'm not saying the kids are phonies—I'm just saying that church is just another social club. The kids in the youth group hang around together at school and go to the same parties. There isn't one bit of difference between the kids in our youth group and the rest of the kids in school. They have sex with their girlfriends or boyfriends, they make fun of people, they swear, they drink, they go to R-rated movies. They do everything that everyone else does, except that they go to church. At church they say all the right things. It's not like they're being hypocrites; it's just that they don't see any problem—you go to church and behave one way, and you go to school and behave another way. I think it's a bunch of baloney. Why even go to church, if it's just another place to go? I don't go anymore. At least I feel more honest.

Carl, 16, Junior

How do you feel about Carl's statement?

| Strongly Agree | Agree | Neutral | Disagree | Strongly Disagree |

▶ If you agree, what would you add to the statement above?

▶ If you disagree, why?

 Scripture Guide: Matthew 5:20   Romans 1:32
                                Luke 11:43   Romans 3:23
                                Romans 1:21–22

33 ■ IMMORAL MAJORITY

I have this friend who goes to a real conservative church that supports the Moral Majority. His youth group decided to protest the sale of *Playboy* and *Penthouse* at the local mini-mart. So they had this big demonstration, and it worked—the store decided to quit selling those magazines. I think that was stupid. I'm against pornography, but what's wrong with *Playboy* and *Penthouse*? We see just as much nudity in most of the movies we go to. And, besides, I don't think we should force people to believe like us.

Shannon, 14, Freshman

How do you feel about Shannon's statement?

| Strongly Agree | Agree | Neutral | Disagree | Strongly Disagree |

▶ If you agree, what would you add to the statement above?

▶ If you disagree, why?

● Scripture Guide: Genesis 1:27   1 Corinthians 6:13
                    Genesis 4:7   1 Corinthians 6:18
                                          2 Corinthians 12:21

34 ■ JUST WAITING

Yes, I like the fact that my folks have money. I like having a car, a nice house, and nice clothes. I enjoy all of those things. But if my parents think I'm going to be like them, they're wrong. I've made up my mind that, when I get older, I'm not going to do the big American Dream thing. I'm not going to get a job so I can buy a house in suburbia, get my Volvo station wagon, and have 2.3 kids. As soon as I get out of college, I'm going to some third-world country, live in a tent, and give my life to helping people. I enjoy the good things in life, but I also hate what they do to me and my parents. I'm not going to let that happen. My folks would die if they knew how I really felt, so I don't tell them. I'm just waiting until I'm old enough to do what I want.

Ken, 16, Sophomore

How do you feel about Ken's statement?

Strongly Agree	Agree	Neutral	Disagree	Strongly Disagree

▶ If you agree, what would you add to the statement above?

▶ If you disagree, why?

 Scripture Guide: Matthew 19:16–24   Ephesians 6:1–3
                   Luke 6:24   Revelation 3:17

SECTION THREE

TENSIONS

The stories in this section require your youth group to rank each character in a story and to provide reasons for those rankings.

35 ■ LIKE FATHER, LIKE DAUGHTER

Kirsten's father was an alcoholic. For now, Mr. Jorgensen was working—although he had lost many jobs over the last few years. Mr. Jorgensen was an after-work drinker. He would stop at a local bar on his way home from work and then come home and drink until he passed out in front of the television.

Kirsten never knew what to expect from him. Sometimes he would be angry and would verbally abuse anyone who was in the same room with him. Other times, he'd be very depressed. Then he would tearfully apologize to Kirsten and promise never to drink again. He would promise to take her shopping the next day and buy her lots of new clothes. But the promises were never kept.

Kirsten didn't know what to think of her mother. Most of the time she was very understanding. She would make excuses for her father and tuck him in at night. She never mentioned his drinking problems to others. But it was strange: Every time Kirsten's father would *stop* drinking, her mother would become bitter. She would yell at him constantly, belittling him and calling him a loser and a weakling, telling him about all the embarrassment and pain he had caused Kirsten and her. She would complain about the lack of money and accuse him of drinking their happiness away. So Kirsten's father would start drinking again, and Mrs. Jorgensen would again become the perfect example of a loving and devoted wife.

Kirsten hated her father's drinking, and it was true that his drinking had cost the family a lot—but she also hated the way her mother acted when her father would try to stop drinking. Kirsten wondered, sometimes, whether her mother *wanted* her father to drink. She felt terrible for thinking such a thing, but she couldn't rid herself of those thoughts. Kirsten and her mother never talked about her father and his drinking. Once Kirsten suggested that they all go for counseling. Her mother flew into a rage and told Kirsten that it was her father who was sick, not them. They didn't need any help. Kirsten never brought it up again.

Kirsten tried to find help anyway. She went to her school counselor, who told her that alcoholism was a disease and that what her father needed was understanding, love, and medical help. *Fine*, Kirsten thought, *but if it's just a disease, then why doesn't my father get medical help?* Kirsten went to her youth director at church. He said alcoholism was not a disease, it was a sin. He said the best thing Kirsten could do would be to pray for her father and get him to come to church. She tried. He wouldn't come.

Kirsten cared a lot for her father, but she had her own life to lead too. Kirsten felt pretty lucky to have a boyfriend like Rick. He was always there when she needed him, and lately she had needed him a lot. They were involved sexually, and that was because of Kirsten, not Rick. She needed the sexual closeness. When she and Rick had sex, she felt like all her problems were gone and the only thing that mattered was she and Rick. Rick was everything. She knew she loved him and that eventually they would get married. That's why she wasn't prepared when Rick said it was over. He said it was just that he wanted some space—that he didn't want to be so serious for a while. But Kirsten didn't believe him. She pled with him to tell her what was really wrong. Finally, in frustration, Rick said that he was sick of her, that she smothered him. He was also tired of listening to her go on and on about her family problems. But the most painful thing he said was: "I hate sex with you. It's like you're using me. It's like sex is a drug, or something to help you escape from your problems. Well, I'm tired of being used, and I'm tired of you."

Kirsten was devastated. She didn't know people could hurt so much. She left school and ran home. No one was there. She was almost hysterical, and that frightened her. She didn't know what to do. And then she considered doing something she thought she would never do—resort to drinking. It would calm her down. She didn't even like the stuff, and one time surely couldn't hurt her. She found the wine in the refrigerator and poured herself a glass. It went down easier than she thought. She did feel better. She had one more and then another. Mrs. Jorgensen came home at four in the afternoon. Kirsten was asleep on the couch (passed out, actually) with an almost empty bottle of wine on the floor.

▶ Rank the following characters as to who was most responsible for Kirsten's drinking problem: Kirsten, Mr. Jorgensen, Mrs. Jorgensen, School Counselor, Youth Director, Rick.

▶ Provide a reason for each of the rankings.

 Scripture Guide: Deuteronomy 21:20–21   1 Timothy 5:23
Ephesians 6:2   Titus 1:7
Ephesians 6:4   Titus 2:3–4

36 ■ CLOSE CALL

It had been a very close call. Teresa and Bill had been going together for three years now, and both of them were still virgins. That could have ended tonight. Luckily, they'd been interrupted by another couple coming to the same spot.

Teresa was so upset she couldn't sleep. She really liked Bill a lot, and when she got married (which would be a long time from now) she wouldn't mind marrying a guy like Bill. He was thoughtful, kind, intelligent (he could actually talk about something other than football and partying), and he wasn't pushy. Teresa believed that sex before marriage was wrong, but she also believed that getting pregnant was worse. She didn't believe in abortion, and the thought of having a baby in high school was more than she could handle.

Teresa decided to be honest with her parents and talk about what she should do. She had always been very open with her parents; they'd been able to talk about everything. Teresa talked to her mom first: "Mom, I'm getting worried. Bill and I have been getting pretty serious and, well, you know, we've kinda been getting carried away sexually. We haven't done anything yet, so don't panic, but I'm afraid we might. Should I think about birth control, Mom?"

Mrs. Dehan replied, "Teresa, you know how much your father and I like Bill. And we like the idea of the two of you going together. The fact that you told me about your sexual problems tells me that you know what's wrong, and I have faith in both of you that you won't violate what you know is right. Besides, if both of you just pray before you go out on a date, I believe God will protect you from going too far. I don't believe in birth control before marriage, Teresa, and I don't think you should use any."

Teresa's father surprised her. He suggested that she and Bill break up for a while to let things cool off. He said that, if they really loved each other, they could wait until they were both older. Teresa didn't like that answer at all.

At youth group that week, the discussion was about birth control. Todd, the youth director, said that using birth control was like planning to sin. It was deciding that you probably would have sex. Todd said that it was just a myth that all couples had sex, and that lots of kids waited until marriage to have sex. Birth control was like saying that sex was inevitable, and planning on sex before marriage was condoning it.

Bill and Teresa had a long talk that evening after youth group. They decided that sex between them was definitely wrong, and that they would take extra precautions to make sure they didn't get into a situation where sex might be possible. But, secretly, Teresa had already made up her mind. She was going to have some kind of birth control. She decided to go to a Planned Parenthood clinic where she could receive any kind of birth control she wanted. She decided on the pill.

Two months later, the impossible happened. One afternoon after school, Bill and Teresa stopped by her house to change clothes for a swim party, and suddenly they were in Teresa's bedroom having sex. Her parents were at work.

Bill panicked. Tearful and apologetic, he told Teresa that if she got pregnant she would have to get an abortion. Teresa couldn't believe it. Bill was against abortion—he *hated* abortions. Trying to calm him down, Teresa explained that there was no fear of her getting pregnant because she was on the pill.

But that made Bill even more upset. He accused Teresa of planning the whole afternoon. He couldn't believe she was on the pill when they both had agreed not to use it. Teresa responded, "Well, it's a good thing I *was* on the pill, or I might have had to face pregnancy alone, because you would have wanted me to get an abortion!"

"Teresa, if you lied about this, who knows what else you've been lying about! Maybe you've been on the pill a lot longer than I know. Maybe I'm not the only one—" Bill didn't finished his sentence. He knew he'd gone too far.

Through her tears, Teresa told Bill to get out and never come back. He tried to apologize, but it was too late. He left. Neither of them officially broke up. They just never saw each other again.

▶ Rank the following characters in the story from best to worst: Teresa, Bill, Mrs. Dehan, Mr. Dehan, Youth Director.

▶ Provide a reason for each of the rankings.

● Scripture Guide: Genesis 4:7   Ephesians 5:1
                     Romans 14:13   Ephesians 5:31
                     1 Corinthians 6:18–19   Colossians 3:5

37 ■ ONE MISTAKE

Trent had definitely made a mistake. He had gone out with the guys and got drunk. He knew he shouldn't have, but sometimes things just got to him and he needed to escape. Drinking was his escape from his parent's divorce. At least that's what he always told himself. There'd been other times, of course, but this was the first time he'd been caught.

His punishment was restriction for a month from all activities and from use of the car. That was okay. He could handle that. He deserved it.

But there was another problem: Ever since the night he'd got caught, his father and stepmother had changed. They didn't trust him anymore. He'd expected that for a while, but it was going on too long. They never *said* they didn't trust him, of course; they would just check up on him all the time. They didn't believe him when he was late or when he explained why he had changed his plans. They continued to believe that he was cheating or lying to them. After a while, Trent told himself that it wouldn't matter *what* he did anymore, since his parents always believed the worst anyway. It was an inconvenience, but not much more than that—until last Tuesday night.

Trent invited his best friend, Eric, to spend the night with him at his real mother's house. She was going to be out of town for a couple of days. They planned to go crazy with movies. They told Trent's father they were going to a movie at the local theater and then they were going to rent a video and watch it at his mother's house. His father asked whether they were going to have any girls over; Trent said no.

Later, on his way to the store, Trent's father passed by his ex-wife's house. Eric's car was there—which meant that Eric and Trent had not gone to the movies. Later, as he was returning from the store, he noticed that Eric's car was now gone. He drove downtown and found Eric's car in front of the video store. He parked his car and waited for them to leave. They left the store, crossed the street to a liquor store, came out with a full, large brown bag, jumped back in the car and returned home.

Trent's father went on back home. By now he was very suspicious. The boys *had* said they were going to rent a video—but they had also said they were going to the theater, which they had not. And what kind of refreshments had they bought at the liquor store? As the evening wore on, he grew more and more uneasy. Finally, convinced that something was up, he decided to drive slowly by his ex-wife's house just to see if anything looked suspicious.

As he drove past, he noticed a station wagon pull up next door. Trent's father parked his car and turned out the lights. Five girls jumped out of the station wagon and walked up to the front door of Trent's house, knocked, and went inside. Trent's father couldn't believe what he was seeing. About thirty seconds later, all the girls came out of the house, got back in the station wagon and drove off.

Angry now, Trent's dad barged inside, where he found Trent and Eric watching a video. "Okay, guys, I've nailed you this time. You didn't go the movie like you said."

"Yes, we did!"

"No, you didn't! Your car was right here. I saw it."

"I know, Dad—that's because we walked to the movie."

"But when I came by later, your car was gone!"

"That's because Eric left his wallet in the car and we needed his money to rent a video."

"Yeah, but you did go to the liquor store and you did have some girls over. You lied to me and I don't like it."

Trent stood up. "That's not true, Dad. The girls came over because they saw Eric's car in front of the house and they wanted us to go cruisin' with them. I told them we couldn't have any girls over or go anywhere with them, so they left. Ask Eric." Trent knew that his dad would believe Eric. Embarrassed, Trent's dad apologized and left the two boys.

Relieved, Eric said that he'd really thought they were busted and that he couldn't believe that Trent's father would actually admit that he was wrong and apologize—after all, *his* father had never done that.

But Trent was furious. He didn't care whether his father had apologized or not. He said he was sick of his father holding one mistake over his head the rest of his life. He was angry at his dad for making a scene in front of his friend. "Fine," he said. "If my dad thinks he can't trust me, then I might as well give him something to not trust me about. Call up the girls, Eric—we're going to have a party right now. And see if any of them can get some beer."

Eric went along with it. Actually, he'd always wanted to drink and party, but he'd never had the chance. Now, here it was—and he could always blame Trent if he was caught.

▶ Rank the following characters in the story from best to worst: Trent, Eric, Trent's dad.

▶ Provide a reason for each of the rankings.

● Scripture Guide: Colossians 3:13–14   1 Thessalonians 4:1
                    Colossians 3:20–21

38 ■ THE SEARCH

Paul's mother was searching his room when she heard Paul at the front door. She had found a bong hidden in his closet, but no pot. She had decided to search his room when she'd overheard him talking to a friend on the phone about being wasted. She was shocked. She had never dreamed this would happen to her son. This only happened to other people's kids.

She ran out to meet Paul in the hallway, holding the bong. Paul panicked—How did his mother find that? This wasn't supposed to happen. She was ruining everything. Why couldn't she leave him alone and let him make his own decisions? He didn't interfere with *her* life. He didn't say anything to her about the wine she drank at dinner or the types of men she dated. What gives her the right to tell *him* how to live? After all, Paul was seventeen years old.

Hysterically, she asked Paul what the "thing," as she called it, was doing in his closet. She threw it against the wall; it broke into a hundred pieces. Paul said nothing. His mother began crying uncontrollably. Paul walked into his room. It was a mess. His mother had gone through everything.

When she stopped crying, she walked into Paul's room and sat down next to him on the bed. She explained to him that she had searched his room because she loved him very much. She needed the truth from him—that was very important to her and to their relationship. She tried to tell Paul that she understood how difficult things had been since the divorce. His father, who had moved out of state for business reasons, had not visited him for over three years. She wanted to know how she could make it up to him.

Paul decided to tell his mother the truth about the bong. It wasn't really his; he was keeping it for a friend. The two of them had been smoking a few bowls of pot on the weekends for the past three months. His dope smoking was under control. He told his mother she had nothing to worry about. He smoked pot like she drank wine. He wouldn't become drug dependent, just like she wouldn't become an alcoholic.

His mom hit the roof. Screaming, she told Paul that he'd have to see a drug counselor or move out of the house.

And Paul had thought that telling the truth would get him off the hook. So much for telling the truth.

The drug counselor felt that Paul had a serious drug problem, and that he was doing more drugs than he admitted. He recommended that Paul be placed in a residential drug treatment center.

After listening to the advice of the counselor, Paul's mother told Paul that he had the choice of entering the treatment center or moving out of the house.

Paul's father, when Paul called him to explain, said that it might be best for Paul if he came to live with him. Paul decided to move in with his dad.

▶ Rank the following characters from best to worst: Paul, Paul's father, Paul's mother, the drug counselor.

▶ Provide a reason for each of the rankings.

 Scripture Guide: Proverbs 22:6   Ephesians 6:1–4
                    Romans 1:30   Colossians 3:20
                    1 Corinthians 6:19–20

39 ■ LESS THAN PERFECT

Chuck rushed his wife, Diane, to the hospital. Her contractions were coming closer and closer together. The day they'd been so patiently awaiting had finally arrived—the birth of their first child. Despite his nervousness and excitement, Chuck couldn't think of a happier moment in his life. Both he and Diane desperately wanted a child.

But afterwards, the obstetrics nurse had some painful news. The newborn baby girl had a genetic defect that was not correctable. The infant had visible deformities and moderate-to-severe brain damage. Chuck and Diane were devastated. Diane wanted to hold her baby. Chuck said no.

Then the doctor hurried into the room, a pained look on his face. "This is never an easy thing to discuss," he said in a low voice. He gave them a progress report: The baby might live, but it most definitely would not live a normal life. Medical care would be expensive. Chuck and Diane didn't have insurance coverage for all the costs of the necessary care. As they talked, the doctor wondered whether he should tell Diane and Chuck any more. Maybe he should let the child die without asking their permission. On the other hand, maybe he should do everything within his power to keep the child alive. But he finally suggested to Diane and Chuck that they allow the infant to die. If they agreed, the hospital's normal procedure was to discontinue medical care and feeding of the infant.

At first Diane disagreed, but Chuck insisted that they follow the doctor's advice. Reluctantly, she went along with Chuck's decision. The doctor placed the order on the baby's medical chart. The obstetrics nurse, when she saw the doctor's orders, strongly disagreed—she felt the doctor was murdering an innocent, helpless child. She was quietly taken off the case. The baby died two days later.

► Rank the following characters from best to worst: Chuck, Diane, the doctor, the baby, the obstetrics nurse.

► Provide a reason for each of the rankings.

● Scripture Guide:　Genesis 1:27　　　　　John 9:2−3
　　　　　　　　　　　Psalms 139:13−16

40 ■ PARTYING

"*Of course* there'll be alcohol, Pam. It's going to be a *party*." Jeff handed Pam the map and walked to class.

Pam closed her locker and headed for class. *Why does partying always have to include drinking?* she wondered. She'd probably go, since everyone she knew would be there. *It'll be all right, since I don't drink. Besides, the last party was fun. Jerri was there, and she acted so funny when she was drunk.*

Pam's parents didn't like her going to parties where there was alcohol. But they didn't need to know about the booze. She wouldn't lie to them, but she wouldn't volunteer any information either.

When Pam got home that afternoon, she found a postcard from her church reminding her of the upcoming youth group social—the same night as Jeff's party. Her parents would encourage—no, would *pressure* her into attending the church social, which Pam knew would be boring. She wished her parents would get off her back about church things.

The day of the party, Pam's parents asked her what time she'd be home from the church social. She told them she wasn't in the mood for church activities and would prefer to go out with her girlfriends. Her parents reluctantly agreed. Pam went to the party with her girlfriends. Maybe she could keep them from getting too drunk.

▶ Rank the following characters from the best to worst: Jeff, Pam, Jerri, Pam's parents, Pam's girlfriends.

▶ Provide a reason for each of the rankings.

 Scripture Guide: Romans 16:17   Hebrews 10:25
                            Ephesians 6:4   1 Peter 2:11–12
                            1 Thessalonians 5:22

41 ■ X-RATED

Kurt couldn't believe his eyes. Right there in the middle of the living room, *his* living room, was an X-rated movie on the TV. "Hey, Kurt," said Mike, his older brother, "me and the guys are putting the new VCR to good use while Mom's at work." Several of Mike's friends were scattered around the room. Mike smirked. "Oh, come on, Kurt, don't look at me like that. Jack here enlisted in the Navy, and we figured this would be a good send-off party for him." Jack, sprawled across the couch, was grinning. "Hey, it's only a movie," Mike continued. "It's no big deal. Mom'll never find out if you don't tell her. So why don't you get lost for the afternoon—and don't give me any of that Christian stuff."

As Kurt left the house he could hear Mike and his friends laughing. He was ready to give up on his brother. He was a hopeless case. Mike used to go to church and youth group meetings. He'd even been president of the youth group once. But something had happened to Mike, and Kurt didn't know what it could have been. It hadn't been his parents. They had done everything they could for Mike.

The next day, Mike apologized to Kurt and asked him again not to tell their mother. He promised it wouldn't happen again. *Sure*, Kurt thought. *I've heard that before.* He walked out of the room.

▶ Rank the following characters from best to worst: Kurt, Mike, Mike's friends, Jack.

▶ Provide a reason for each of the rankings.

 Scripture Guide: Matthew 6:14–15   1 Corinthians 6:18
                    Luke 6:32   1 Peter 2:11
                    Romans 13:8

42 ■ THE DIARY

Michelle's mother found the diary accidently while she was cleaning Michelle's closet. She knew she shouldn't read it, but her curiosity got the better of her, and the next thing she knew she was reading her daughter's diary.

She was stunned. She could not believe that her daughter had written such things. She didn't think her daughter was capable of such anger toward her parents. Mrs. Carson had always thought she and her daughter had a great relationship, but the things her daughter had said about her after some of their arguments shocked her. There was so much—too much to take at one time. She had no idea her daughter had ever had anything to drink, let alone got drunk. And the things she said about her dates. Did kids really do things like that nowadays? Her own daughter? It was horrible. And the language. Mrs. Carson had no idea her daughter ever used any swear words, let alone the ones she so freely used in her diary. Where had she learned such things?

Mrs. Carson showed Michelle's diary to her husband. He was furious, all right—but not with Michelle. He was furious with his wife for reading the diary. Still, he was shocked at what was in it. He didn't read it, but Mrs. Carson had told him enough. Even though he believed Michelle's privacy had been violated, he also believed that something needed to be done about Michelle. How could they, as respectable parents, ignore what they knew?

The Carsons went to see their minister. They didn't bring the diary, but they did tell him they knew what was in it. The pastor affirmed Mrs. Carson's decision to read the diary. He believed that whatever parents have to do to help their child grow up is okay. If that means going through their drawers, their clothes, or their diaries to make sure they are telling the truth and not in trouble, then that's okay. "Parents have the right," the pastor said, "to do whatever it takes to protect their children from the rough world out there."

The Carsons went home and confronted their daughter. Michelle completely fell apart. She couldn't believe that her own parents would violate her privacy and read her diary. The argument became so heated and ugly that Michelle left and went to stay with a friend. Her parents had no idea where she'd gone, but neither of them felt the least regret for what they had done; the fact that Michelle ran away only confirmed that they had done the right thing. *Michelle knew she was wrong*, they reasoned, *and that is why she ran away. She'll be back.*

▶ Rank the following characters in the story from best to worst: Michelle, Mrs. Carson, Mr. Carson, Minister.

▶ Provide a reason for each of the rankings.

● Scripture Guide: Colossians 3:20   2 Timothy 3:1—5
                      1 Timothy 3:4—5

43 ■ SECRET BIRTH CONTROL

Robin didn't sleep around. She *did* sleep with her boyfriend, but that wasn't "sleeping around." It wasn't promiscuous—she really *loved* her boyfriend. She hoped someday they would get married. Sure, Seth wasn't the only boyfriend she had slept with, but people who love each other *should* have sex together. Sex is part of love.

Robin was eighteen and a senior—old enough to make her own decisions. She had always tried to be honest with her parents. That doesn't mean she told them everything; there was such a thing as timing. Now that she was eighteen, she decided it was the right time to have a frank discussion with her parents (well, her mom anyway). She told her mom that she thought it was okay to have sex with someone you love and that, in fact, she had been having sex with Seth. She also told her mother that she thought abortion was wrong and therefore wanted to have birth control. Her mother was appalled at the whole conversation and refused to even discuss the possibility of birth control. She ordered Robin to break up with Seth and to not have sex with anyone. Robin reminded her mother that she could order birth control pills without her permission. Her mother threatened to destroy any birth control pills or devices she found.

Robin continued having sex with Seth and acquired birth control pills through a local clinic. A couple of months later her mother found the pills and threw them away. Robin was so angry that she continued to have sex with Seth without any protection. Two months later she discovered she was pregnant. Since she didn't believe in abortion, she told Seth that she was pregnant, fully expecting him to agree to get married. After all, they had been talking about it. She was shocked to discover he had no intention of getting married and blamed her for getting pregnant in the first place.

"If you had used birth-control pills, we wouldn't be in this mess," he told her.

"Well, what about *you!*" she yelled. "Why didn't *you* use protection?"

Seth replied sarcastically, "Because *I'm* not the one who can get pregnant!"

Robin broke up with Seth and had an abortion. All her parents knew was that she had broken up with Seth. They were very proud of Robin and glad to see that she had responded to their wishes.

▶ Who was most responsible for Robin's abortion?

▶ Rank the following characters from most responsible to least responsible: Robin, Seth, Robin's mom.

▶ Provide a reason for each of the rankings.

● Scripture Guide: Psalms 139:13–16   1 Corinthians 6:18–20
                     Proverbs 22:6   Ephesians 6:1–4
                     1 Corinthians 6:13

44 ■ THE END OF A FUTURE

The "animals." That's what everyone at school called them. Barry, Brad, Aaron, Jim, and Ken were all seniors. Their contribution to the football team was vital if the team was to win the league championship—which everyone expected, even though the season was just beginning.

Despite the fact that Barry's parents were alcoholics, he was a 3.8 student and was already being recruited by a number of big-time colleges. His parents were unemployed, but Barry was looking forward to a full-ride scholarship.

Though Brad was considered one of the "animals," he was a lot different than the rest of them. He didn't drink or party. Brad was a committed Christian and had the respect of all the other guys.

The Tuesday night before the season opener, the "animals" decided to have a secret drinking party to celebrate the beginning of a great season. All of them except Brad, that is. The guys knew Brad wouldn't drink—but they needed him for an alibi. Their parents trusted Brad, and if they said they were going to Brad's, no questions would be asked. Brad didn't like the idea, but he said he'd go along with it as long as the guys agreed to let him drive. They said no. They had too much respect for Brad to want him around while they got drunk. Brad agreed to cover for them, but he didn't like it.

On the way home from the party Tuesday night, Barry's car was pulled over by the police. All of the guys were hauled down to the police station, and their parents were called. The football coach heard about it the next day and angrily dropped all the "animals" from the team. Barry's future was ruined. The schools that were recruiting him suddenly lost interest. He became so depressed he began drinking every weekend. His grades fell, and eventually he dropped out of school and became an alcoholic, just like his parents.

Brad went on to college, but he was never the same. He blamed himself for Barry's disastrous one-night drinking binge. He dropped out of church and became a real loner.

▶ Who is most responsible for Barry's alcoholism?

▶ Rank the following characters from most responsible to least responsible: Barry, Brad, Barry's parents, the football coach.

▶ Provide a reason for each of the rankings.

 Scripture Guide: Psalms 37:25   Matthew 18:6
                     Proverbs 20:1   Romans 2:9
                     Matthew 5:13   Galatians 5:21

45 ■ THE QUITTER

Bob, a high-school senior, received a car for his eighteenth birthday. His parents told him he'd have to pay for the gas and insurance for the car himself—he'd been working at a fast-food restaurant for almost a year. If it weren't for that, they wouldn't have been able to afford the car.

What they didn't know was that Bob hated his job. He was making minimum wage, and his bosses were *treating* him like a minimum-wage employee, making him do all the jobs that the higher-paid employees didn't want to do. He was always at the bottom of the totem pole when it came to scheduling, as well. They would often tell him he had to work Friday and Saturday nights, and then when he showed up, tell him they needed him for only an hour or they didn't need him at all. When work was extra busy, they'd make him stay late and close the restaurant because the higher-paid employees "had plans." Bob had been planning to quit for a long time. Of course, he was excited about the car—but he also wanted to quit his job.

After he'd had the car a month, he told his parents he wanted to quit work. His parents were very upset. Bob explained that he was being mistreated at work and that his bosses refused to listen to his complaints. But his parents insisted that they bought the car with the expectation that Bob would pay for its upkeep. "It's too late," Bob shrugged. "I already gave notice." His father angrily called Bob's boss, who told him that if Bob hadn't given notice to quit, he would have been fired for his terrible attitude and his laziness.

Furious now, Bob's dad accused Bob of being irresponsible, lazy, and selfish—and dishonest, because he misled his parents until after they bought the car. "If you quit your job," he said, "I'll sell the car."

Bob, devastated, insisted that his boss wasn't telling the truth. "I'm *not* lazy," he told his father. "I just don't like being treated like a slave. And remember—I worked six months longer than I wanted to, just to prove that I'm not lazy or irresponsible."

His parents refused to accept his explanation. "The real world out there isn't very friendly," they explained condescendingly. "Many people have to work at jobs they don't like. Sometimes adults have to do what they don't want to do just to survive."

"I understand all that," Bob said. "But sometimes you have to stand up to people who mistreat you. I don't want to ignore my responsibilities; I just want to be treated like a human being."

His parents gave him an ultimatum: Work or no car. Bob quit his job. His parents sold the car.

▶ Rank the following characters in this story from best to worst: Bob, Bob's parents, Bob's boss.

▶ Provide a reason for each of the rankings.

 Scripture Guide: Ephesians 6:4   Colossians 3:20–21
Ephesians 6:7   Colossians 3:23
Colossians 3:17

46 ■ FATSO

Jenay was basically a happy girl—a junior in high school, good looking, slim. Everything was going great until the end of her junior year, and then the bottom fell out. Not only were her parents divorced, but her mother remarried almost immediately. Everyone at school knew about the divorce and knew that Jenay's mom was involved with another guy *before* the divorce. Jenay didn't get along well with her real father, but she *hated* Gary, her new stepfather. She understood why her mother wanted to get a divorce, but after she met Gary, her mother had no time for Jenay—all she could think about was him. Jenay felt that she was in the way, and when she would ask her mother about it, her mother would simply say that Jenay was overreacting and not being very understanding.

Jenay thought about going to live with her real father but decided against it for a number of reasons. First, she didn't get along with her father, although she did feel sorry for him because her mom had been unfaithful. And second, Jenay's mother had made it very clear that if Jenay went with her father, it would be considered a betrayal.

Jenay was depressed a lot. And she quickly discovered that eating helped. She didn't notice it at first, but slowly, gradually, she realized she was eating all the time and gaining weight. Lots of weight. The more weight she gained, the more Jenay's mom complained. There were times when her mother threatened to send Jenay to her father's if she didn't stop. In fact, Jenay called her father and asked whether she could live with him. He said no—he had his own life to live, and besides, if she was as heavy as everyone said then she had better quit worrying about where to live and start losing weight instead.

Jenay just kept eating. One day her church youth director stopped by and told Jenay that he was concerned about her. Jenay felt like she could trust him, so she told him all about the family problems that had led to her overeating. He told Jenay that all she needed to do was pray and ask God to take away the desire to eat. Jenay did pray for about six months—she gained another five pounds.

At least she still had her boyfriend. She'd been going steady with Martin for almost two years. She was relieved that he still cared for her despite her weight problem. They'd been sexually active almost from the beginning. Then the worst happened—Jenay found a note in Martin's car that he had written to a friend. It said:

Bob, I've got to figure out how to dump Jenay, quick. I've wanted to get rid of Fatso for a long time but I didn't want to hurt her feelings and, besides, the sex is great.

The next day Jenay swallowed a whole bottle of sleeping pills.

▶ Who was most responsible for Jenay's inability to cope with life?

▶ Rank the following characters from most responsible to least responsible: Jenay, Martin, Jenay's mother, Jenay's real father, Jenay's stepfather, Jenay's youth director.

▶ Provide a reason for each of the rankings.

● Scripture Guide: Romans 12:9–10   Ephesians 6:4
                   Romans 13:10   Colossians 3:20–21
                   1 Corinthians 9:27

SECTION FOUR

DEAR DIARY

These fictional "diary entries" are intimate, no-holds-barred statements of adolescent feelings. Have your youth group read these "confidential" writings and then respond to them.

47 ■ HEARTTHROB

Dear Diary,

Today was so great! Jason Ling wants to go steady. He is a totally buff guy. *And he's a senior!* I can't believe it. Any girl in school would give her virginity away for him—and he likes me. I am soooooooo happy. Heather is totally jealous and being a real jerk. I don't care. Of course, it's going to take some real doing to pull this off. You know why! My parents are the nerds of the universe! They don't want me dating seniors. My parents actually think every senior guy wants to rape every freshman girl. Well, they're wrong. Jason is the neatest guy I have ever met and I am not going to let him go. I mean, I wouldn't even mind having sex with him, he turns me on so much. What's wrong with having sex with someone you really like? Nothing. And besides, if I'm going to keep him around for four years, we can't exactly hold hands. Seriously, Diary, I would marry him right now. Of course I can't, I'm only fifteen—but my mom was eighteen when she married my dad. Whoops, gotta go, Jason's calling.

Darla

▶ What should Darla do?

▶ What should Darla's parents do?

▶ What would you do?

 Scripture Guide: 1 Corinthians 6:13   Ephesians 5:3
                                   1 Corinthians 6:18   Colossians 3:5−6
                                   Galatians 5:19−21

48 ■ TOTALLY UGLY

Dear Diary,

Me again. The ugliest girl in high school. You know how many dates I've had in high school in four years? Zero. Zip. None! Every other person in the world dates, or has a boyfriend. Do you know how ugly you have to be to get no dates, no boyfriends? My parents are so dumb. They're always telling me how great I am. Know why? Because I get straight A's and now I get a scholarship to go to college so they don't have to pay anything. They don't even care about my social life. They actually act like it doesn't matter if I date as long as I get good grades. I hate school. I hate being smart. I would much rather have a boyfriend like Mike Carillo or Darin Johnston and be totally stupid. I wish I was dead. Really!

Oh, and you know what else! They keep telling me that it doesn't matter how you look, it's what's inside. Right. Trouble is, no one in the entire universe believes that. Besides, that tells me what they think of me. They *do* think I'm ugly! There is nothing worse than being ugly. Nothing.

Corrie

▶ What advice would you give Corrie?

▶ What advice would you give Corrie's parents?

▶ What would you do if you were Corrie?

● Scripture Guide: Genesis 1:27   Luke 12:7
                      Matthew 10:31

49 ■ NO BIG DEAL

Dear Diary,

I can't believe how freaked all my friends are about *AIDS*. Give me a break! They act like we're all going to get it. First of all, you can't get *AIDS* unless you are some kind of homosexual, do drugs, or sleep around all the time with a million different people. My minister at church actually said tonight that the best way to protect yourself from *AIDS* is not to have sex with anyone except the person you are going to marry. So how do you know that the person you are marrying didn't have sex with someone? Dumb. I think the safest thing you can do is have sex with other high-school kids, because they really aren't that experienced with sex. They usually just have sex with other high-school kids. I think that's great. In fact, the safest thing you can do is go steady with the same person all through high school and then marry her. Most of my friends would say the same thing, if they're honest.

Darin

▶ Do you agree or disagree with Darin? Explain.

▶ Do you agree or disagree with Darin's minister? Explain.

● Scripture Guide: Romans 6:23   Ephesians 5:3
                      1 Corinthians 6:13 Colossians 2:20–23
                      1 Corinthians 6:18–20

50 ■ THE JERK

Dear Diary,

Why is my brother such a jerk? He's always using my stuff, ruining my tapes, and losing half my clothes. My parents think he's just the most wonderful person in the whole world, and that *I'm* the trouble-maker. If they only knew. He lies to them all the time, he uses their credit cards without their permission, he drinks like a fish—and my parents think he's Mr. Innocent! I can't believe it. Sometimes I hate my brother, and other times I feel sorry for him. He's so selfish. He uses them. He uses me. So how come I don't let my parents know the truth about him? Because I'm not a narc. And anyway, my parents wouldn't believe me. I'm going to be real glad when he gets out of this house. I wish he were leaving today.

Carl

▶ What advice would you give to Carl?

▶ What advice would you give to Carl's brother?

▶ If Carl's parents had read this diary entry, what would you advise them to do?

 Scripture Guide: Genesis 4:8–10   Ephesians 6:1
                                Genesis 37:17–20   1 John 2:9–11

51 ■ FREAKED OUT FUNERAL

Dear Diary,

Gary Sellstrum got in a giant wreck last night. He ran off the road and was killed. I guess it was pretty horrible. He really got messed up bad. I didn't know him all that well, but he was real popular in school and everyone was freaked out. I bet every girl in school was crying. His funeral is in a couple of days and the school is going to let everyone go. Yuk! Funerals! Horrible. Why would anyone want to go to a funeral? I mean, I didn't even know the guy. I think everyone's going just to get out of school. Maybe they're going because it's the cool thing to do. They didn't really care about Gary and they won't a couple of days from now. Besides, I think funerals are for old people. If you're dead, you're dead. Why sit around and look at a dead body? I would rather have everyone remember me as I was. I'm never going to have a funeral.

Teresa

▶ Do you agree with Teresa's opinion of funerals?

▶ What advice would you give to Teresa?

 Scripture Guide: Ecclesiastes 3:1–2   Hebrews 9:27
                    Ecclesiastes 3:4   Hebrews 10:30
                    Matthew 5:4

52 ■ TEENAGE MOM

Dear Diary,

I don't believe my mother. It's like she thinks she's sixteen or something. I need a million clothes and I come home today and she's totally dressed like a teenager. She looks better than I do! I'm serious. When I say something like I think she looks ridiculous or I think she looks too young, she goes crazy. She gets all mad and says that everyone dresses like that—which they don't. She says that she has the right, after all these years, to buy herself some clothes, and that it's okay for a mom to want to look nice. Gee, Mom, no kidding. She doesn't even listen. It's embarrassing. And she's always wanting me to invite all the "girls" over so *we* can do something together. Can you believe it? I don't want my mom to do things with me and the girls. I've even tried to talk to Dad about it. You know what he says? "I *like* your mom to look young." Totally sick! Why don't they just try and look like a mom and a dad instead of trying to look like they're still in their teens?

Becky

▶ What should Becky do?

▶ What should Becky's mom do?

▶ What would you tell Becky's father?

● Scripture Guide: Romans 12:3   Ephesians 6:4
                    1 Corinthians 13:11 1 Timothy 3:4—5
                    Ephesians 6:2—3

53 ■ SOAP AND SEX

Dear Diary,

My mom totally blew up at me today. Yep, you got it. Soaps. She told me never to watch soaps, but she's always gone, and you know how much I like soaps. It's like I'm addicted. Well, she came home early today from work and caught me. I got the all-time lecture once again. "Don't you know they're bad for you? All they show is sex, sex, sex. Everyone in those soaps is sleeping with someone else." She was really mad this time. I just sat there and agreed with her. I mean, what's the use? I don't really agree with her. I mean, I know they do have a lot of sex and everyone is sleeping with everyone, but I know it isn't real life. I know it's wrong. But I'm not going to watch soaps and then become a pervert. They're just fun to watch. Besides, all the guys are total babes.

Lauren

▶ What should Lauren do?

▶ If you were Lauren's mom, what would you say to Lauren about soaps?

▶ What would you do if you were Lauren?

● Scripture Guide:　1 Corinthians 6:18　　James 4:4
　　　　　　　　　　　Ephesians 5:3–6　　　1 Peter 2:1–3
　　　　　　　　　　　Ephesians 5:11–12　　1 John 2:15

DATE DUE

NOV 28 1990		
APR 30 1991		
NOV 26 1991		
OCT 19 1992		
DEC 03 1994		
APR 23 1998		